PEIRE VIDAL

(c. 1175-1205)

PEIRE VIDAL

translations by

PAUL BLACKBURN

DRAWINGS BY BASIL KING

with an introduction by

GEORGE ECONOMOU

MULCH PRESS   NEW YORK / AMHERST   1972

MULCH PRESS
P. O. Box 426
Amherst, Massachusetts 01002

Table of Contents

INTRODUCTION

Paul Blackburn chose for his major work as translator the poetry of the Provençal troubadours. It was a choice that was good for poetry, good for the troubadours, and good for him. It was a choice made out of a special affinity for them. Because he had the gifts and desire, he *became* one and all of them, as with genius and learning he gave their poems his own voice and new life in a new language. And they gave him something in return; in the art of translation the translated ones have their ways of reciprocating. Time will show—to those who are not already aware of it—that it was a historic choice, for it produced one of the most significant bodies of poetic translation ever achieved in our language: "Blackburn's Provençal" will take its place among Gavin Douglas' *Aeneid*, Golding's *Metamorphoses*, the Homer of Chapman, Pope, and Lattimore, Waley's Japanese, and Pound's Chinese, Italian, and Old English.

Like most students of the troubadours, Blackburn especially admired and enjoyed Peire Vidal—that poet of impossible loves (even within the tradition of *fin amor*), deep loyalties, wild schemes, and terrible misfortunes, if we believe what the *razos* and *vida* (probably compiled in the 14th century) tell us about him. These medieval commentaries and biography, which introduce us to a "character," are most likely as much highly imaginative elaborations of things in the poems as they are historically accurate. But the facts and fictions of Vidal have almost always been inseparable, his poems so individualized that the stranger the legendary aura around them the more credible they seem.

That Peire Vidal wrote with great originality and feeling is something that almost everyone who has written about him remarks at the outset. Perhaps more than in the work of any other troubadour, there is present in his poems a realness of personality that is hard to resist. And technically, he is a superior and interesting poet. But finally, it is his spirit that really attracts us, his courage, his truth, his *integritas*—the purity of his vision, whether he is boasting, complaining, or making love. It is no wonder that Blackburn, in his attack on contemporary Toulouse in the magnificent poem *Sirventes*, invokes Vidal's spirit to join him across

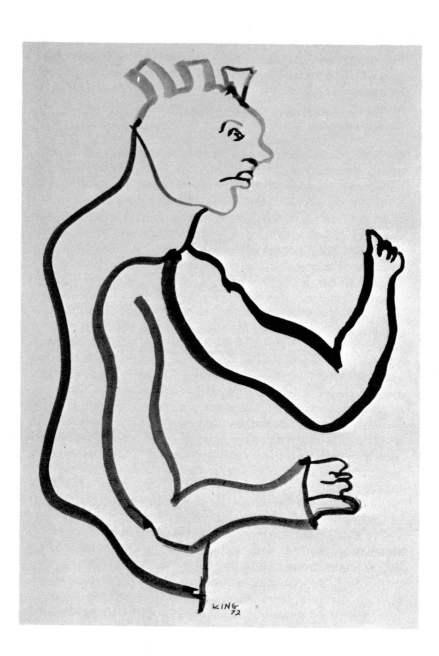

the centuries in showing his contempt and grief for what has become of that city, for what can become of all of us when we abandon that which is distinctive and definitive to ou humanity: "That mad Vidal would spit on it,/ that I as his maddened double/ do—too." For neither Blackburn nor Vidal ever broke the faith of true men and poets. (For a textual basis for the invitation and comparison, see the sixth stanza of *Drogoman senher*, in which Vidal makes some contemptuous remarks about the Toulouse of his own time.)

The seven poems in this volume, five *cansos*, a *vanto*, and a *sirventes* (numbered XVIII, XIX, XII, XIV, X, XXXIV, XXXII, respectively, in Anglade's edition), were all written in *coblas unisonans*, i.e., in stanzas with not only the same rime scheme but with the same end rimes throughout as well. By Provençal standards, it was a popular and fairly easy pattern. Blackburn, of course, elected to *translate the poems* rather than to xerox their formal elements. He writes the translation as if it were his own poem—without betraying either the sense or uniqueness of the original. He writes it with a tone, diction, and cadence that belong to the Vidal poems alone, as distinguished from the other troubadours he has translated—whom he has also rendered with distinctive qualities. That is why these translations are such superb, matchless work: in them Blackburn is even more than poet/translator, he is also something of an actor—in the most creative sense of the word.

Because he was a great poet, translator Blackburn was not afraid to take a risk for the sake of his poet, as in the experiment with intercalated lines in *Estat ai gran sazo*. As for scholarship and erudition, Blackburn always carried it in a quiet, unassuming way; one can see it in his notes to this selection, solid, precise, pertinent, and not too solemn for a joke or two.

Mulch Press, a house of poets and painters, has given us this beautiful book. From their enterprise, Peire Vidal wins, and Paul Blackburn wins. For yours, reader, turn to the poems . . .

George Economou
New York City
June, 1972

PEIRE VIDAL

(c. 1175-1205)

VIDA

Peire Vidal was from Toulouse, the son of a furrier, and sang better than any man in the world. He was one of the maddest fellows who ever lived, for he believed as truth whatever he wanted or whatever happened to please him. And he succeeded in making his songs lighter than anyone else's, and made richer tunes and greater follies of arms and love. And he was apt to speak badly of others. It was true that a knight of St. Gilles had had his, Vidal's tongue cut out, having been given to understand that Peire was his wife's lover. Uc del Bauz took care of him then, and had his tongue treated and cured.

When his tongue had healed he went overseas and brought back with him a Greek girl who'd been given to him as wife on Cyprus. He had been told that she was the niece of the emperor of Constantinople, and given to understand that he, having married her, ought by right to have the empire. Whereupon he put everything he could earn into raising a fleet, intending to go conquer the empire. He went about carrying imperial arms and had his wife called "empress" and himself "the emperor."

He fell in love with all the pretty ladies in sight, and was suitor for all their loves: all told him to do and say whatever he wished, so he believed himself the lover of each of them, and that each was dying for him. All of them deceived him. He was always leading expensive chargers and wearing rich arms, riding with a chair and a tent with imperial insignia. He thought he was the best knight in the world, and the most beloved of the ladies.

13

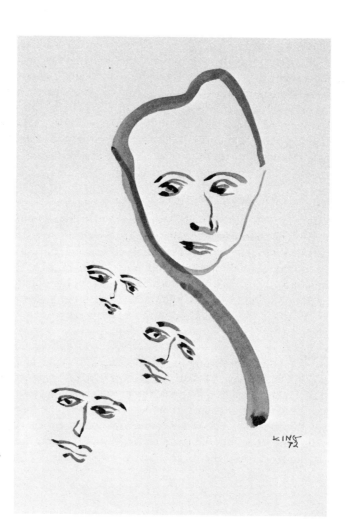

RAZOS

Peire Vidal, as I have told you, was in love with all the lovely ladies, and thought that all of them were in love with him. And now, if you like, I'll tell you how he fell in love with a lady, Alazaïs de Rocamartina, who was the wife of Barrals, lord of Marseille, he who loved Peire Vidal above any man in the world for his rich *trobar* and for the crazy things that he did and said. They called each other mutually "Rainier" and Peire was closer to the court and chamber of en Barrals than any other man in the world.

Indeed, Barrals knew that Peire was in love with his wife, and considered it a pass-time, as did everyone else there who knew of it. He enjoyed the foolishness that Vidal performed and spoke, and the lady accepted it lightly, as did all the other ladies to whom Peire Vidal made love. And each one of them spoke pleasantly to him, and promised him anything that pleased them as well as everything he asked for. And he was so credulous that he swallowed it all. The lady Alazaïs allowed him to court her and beg her love because of the fine *cansos* he made for her, and for the fun she got out of it with him. And she was with him in the court, they dressed like one another, and she presented him with arms. And if Peire Vidal grew angry with her over anything, Barrals immediately made the peace between them, and made her promise him anything he asked for.

Then a day came when Peire Vidal knew that en Barrals had risen early and that the lady was alone in her room. He entered the room and went to the bed of ma domna Alazaïs and found her sleeping. Kneeling before her, he kissed her on the mouth: she felt the kiss and thought it was Barrals, her husband, and rose laughing. When she looked and saw that it was the mad Vidal, she began to cry out and raised a great clamor. Ladies and girls came running from within when they heard it and asked: "What's this? " Peire Vidal ran out.

The lady sent for her husband and began to tell him how that crazy Peire Vidal had kissed her. And she wanted him to have Vidal killed, and wept and begged him to take his vengeance immediately. Barrals, like the noble and sophisticated person he was, took her and comforted her, and laughed and chided his wife that she had made so much noise over what a fool had done. But he could not chastise her for it, because she might spread the story around, and people would seek and inquire, much to Vidal's harm. So he only made him great threats.

At which point, out of fear, Peire boarded a vessel for Genoa. He stayed there until he went overseas with King Richard, for he was set in the fear that Alazaïs would have him seized. And Alazaïs would have exerted herself more than slightly if she could have found him. In one song he says:

> One sore   I reproach her for,
> she forced me to go overseas
> to rid the region of me,
> at least that's how it looks to me.

And he stayed there for a long time and made many good *cansos* recalling the kiss he'd stolen. And in one *canso* called *Ajostar e lassar* he says that he had from her not the slightest reward

> but a small silk cord, and
> there was another thing:
> I entered her house one morning
> and kissed her like a thief
>   chin and mouth.

And elsewhere he says:

> I would have been more honored than any man born,
> had that stolen kiss been granted me
> and given nicely.

And in still another *canso,* says:

> Love beats me with the sticks I cut myself:
> for one time, in a high and regal room,
> I stole a kiss of which my heart remembers.

16

He was overseas for a long time for he didn't dare return to Provence. And when they saw this, the barons, en Barrals and Uc del Bauz, implored the lady so often that she pardoned him the affair of the kiss and granted it to him as a gift. Barrals sent him letters and greetings, said his vexation was forgotten, and wrote him to come. And Vidal took ship and came back to Provence to Uc del Bauz. En Barrals, as soon as he knew that Peire Vidal was at Les Bauz, mounted horse and went to him and led him back to Marseille where he was welcomed by Alazaïs, and out of graciousness she granted him the kiss that he had stolen from her, of which Peire Vidal made the *canso* that starts:

Since I have returned to Provence

in which he says:

I have won with a great
softness, after long waiting,
that kiss which Love's force
forced me to snatch from my lady.
Now she grants it to me and
finds it pleasing.

17

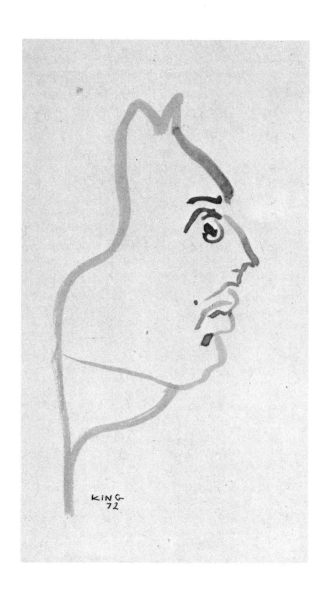

II.

Peire Vidal was in grief over the death of the good count Raimon de Toulouse, and gave himself over to sorrow. He dressed all in black, cut the ears and tails from all his horses, and even had all his servants shave their heads, though they refused to cut their nails or shave off their beards. He went about for a long time mourning like a madman.

And it happened that, during the time he was going about like that, King Alfons of Aragon came up into Provence: and with him came Blascol Romieus, Garcia Romieus, Martin del Canet and Miguel de Luzia, Sans d'Antilon, Guillem d'Alcalla, Albert de Castelvieil, Raimon Gauserans de Pinons, Guillem Raimon de Moncade, Arnaut de Castelbon, and Raimon de Cerveira. And they found Peire Vidal sad and grieving and in this way dressed like a fool. And the king and all the barons protested that they were his special friends, and asked that he leave off grieving and sing and be happy again, and that he should make them a *canso* to take back to Aragon. The king and his barons were so insistent, he said yes he would, put off sorrow and rejoice and make a *canso* and do whatever else might please them.

And he loved besides, Loba de Pennautier, and ma domna Estefania who was from the Cerdanya. And later he was enamoured of ma domna Raimbauda de Biolh. Biolh is in Provence, in the mountains separating Provence from Lombardy. La Loba was from Carcassonne. Peire Vidal called himself Lop because of her, and carried the badge of wolf. In the mountains of Cabaret, shepherds hunted him with dogs, greyhounds and great mastiffs, as if the man were a wolf. In fact he wore a wolfskin, giving that scent to the dogs and their masters. And the shepherds hunted him down with the dogs and beat him so badly that he was taken for dead, and carried to the dwelling of Loba de Pennautier.

And when she knew that this was Peire Vidal, she was greatly amused at the folly he had committed and began to laugh heartily, and her husband likewise. They accepted him with great

19

joy. Her husband had him carried in and laid in a secret place, while they nursed him as best they could. Then he sent for a physician and had him treated until he was well.

As I'd started to tell you, when he had begun to sing and compose *cansos,* as he had promised the king of Aragon and his barons, the king had identical arms made for himself and for Peire Vidal, had clothes made for the both of them: they dressed alike and the king was highly pleased. Peire Vidal then made this *canso* which you shall hear, and which begins:

> I had left off singing in grief
> that my lord count had died.

Plus que·l paubres que jatz el ric ostal

MORE THAN A BEGGAR I dare not
                    grumble,
more than a poor man who sleeps in a rich man's hall
                    who doesn't dare complain
though his complaint be great, fearing
                    his lord take offense, I
dare not grate against my mortal pain
though having for reason her disdain toward me
whom I've wanted more than any,
                    at least that!
          and yet dare not cry mercy—
I fear so to have her angry at me.

When I look upon her in contemplation my
heart so melts, myself entire forgot,
          I stand like a man in ecstasy
                    before a window where beauty is
                    resplendent against the sun.
Love beats me with the sticks I cut myself:
one time, in a high and regal room, I
                    stole a kiss.
                    My heart remembers it.

That makes it now how many Octobers
                    the lady I sing upon these pages
                    has sinned against Love? She
                              neglects me
                              does not aid me
                              still is aware
I've left with her my hope, my heart entire, my love
                    and have no care
          for any other wages.
But why does she signal and welcome me so gently
          if she has no intention
of granting me what the lack of which so pains me?
          I'll suffer again
                    the things that give me pain.

A man ought, with his rightful lord, to pardon all,
if he be wrong or just, wise or a fool.
A man will put himself to some pains in a war
                    to gain honor.
                        But when he's exiled from home
                            it's hard,
                    it takes the fight out of him.
            And if I fall away from loving her,
                    that's the worst exile, but
                            no. I will not.
                I love her now more than before
                and she would only contemn me, were
I to smile at fate and leave off loving.
No fear of that,
for all I am and have I have
only through that loving. And

she has me altogether in her puissance,
                can make me suffer all she likes,
                    I'll not be bitter.
I have so soft a knowledge to do her pleasure
            I lose the memory of my own
                    nor care. No day is
                        my love for her does not
                spring, well up from the heart.
            When we're together and I look on her
such a joy rises in me to the eyes that
                    putting the horse behind the cart
                        my heart
imagines such fine things that in the world there's nothing
else I can
desire or want.

AND SUCH LOVE CUTS THE HEART
FOR I HAVE SEEN NONE more lovely or soft
nor of such bounty. So I have great richness
                loving one who's worth all of it.
            If ever I have the joy to see
            her undressed, alone with me,
I'll be happier than the lord of Excideuil,
who keeps his courage when others but recede.

24

I know of none his equal
saving Geoffrey.

With the four kings of Spain
it all goes badly
since they do not want to make a peace among them—
otherwise it's certain that their valor's great,
they're frank and loyal
courteous and straight,
yet, they still might grace their acts
till they dazzle and gleam,
if they turned their war to another register
and fought
the Saracen who call our religion a joke, FIGHT
until the whole of Spain would be
united under a single faith.
A dream.

Bel Castiat, my lord, in your account, put
me down as one who's sad and over-grave.
The sight of you or Vierna I cannot have
whom I love
from the heart and with a single faith.
A dream.

Ab l'alen tir vas me l'aire

I suck deep in air come from Provence to here.
All things from there so please me
when I hear
in dockside taverns
travelers' gossip told
I listen smiling,
and for each word ask a hundred smiling words,
all news is good

for no man knows so sweet a country as
                          from the Rhône down to Vence.
If only I were locked between
                          Durance and the sea!
Such pure joy shines in the sun there.
          I left my heart-for-rejoicing there
              among noble people,
and with her who bids my sadness dance.

No man can ever pass a day in boredom
                    who has remembrance of her,
for she is the beginning and birth of all joy:
                    and he who would praise her
no matter how well he speaks of her, he lies!
for this world shall not look on one
                          better or fairer.

And if there's anything
I know to say or do, I
merit no praise from it,
for in her is all good
and through her I've wit and knowledge of fulfillment,
so am both poet and happy.
And all I make which has in it any fineness
I have from the rich delight of her fine body,
even as my heart longs for her in straightness.

Una chanso ai faita mortamen

One canso I've made murderously,
so much so
I don't know how I did it.
Evening, morning, day or night
I am not master of my thought,
                              less of my heart.
          Another time when great
          incertitudes were in the balance-pan,
there came to me from Love so overwhelming a
          proof of my luck,
I began to make a canso on the spot.
                         It went like that.

          But why keep me in such a confusion?
She must know that nothing ever pleased me so much.
          From that first hour,
                    the first touch,
I could not split my heart, my love, my mind
                    away from what I'd found. So
that now if she harms me, it's bound to be
                    a disaster for me.
          But if she gives me token
          of accord and friendship, then it's certain
she couldn't offer greater grace or mercy.
And if she need a reason to be right,
          let it
          be that her love sustains me.

But I don't believe at all in her desire, though
she speak and smile and make me promises. No
woman ever lied more agreeably
                         or with such cleverness.
          But I can't help believing when she speaks,
on such peak
of ecstasy
her words put me.

28

But if she speak truth,
not France and I the king of all would make
me feel so happy and peaceful.
But no, she has no heart or good will in the wrangle.

No one ever loved so crazily,
not even he,
the squire who died at table.
I also die
but me she kills more slowly,
and she knows
to do it courteously.
She does not strike with lance or cut with knife
but with soft words and pleasant-seeming welcome.
There you have the weapons she fights me with,
has,
ever since I've known her,
and will
still,
if she keeps me on.

To complete the inventory of her arsenal
I can't forget
beauty, God-given entirely,
nor has he
taken one whit from her:
intelligence, perfect,
perfectly sincere and always gay.
I get this way
because she
does not permit me her love.
Yet they say
one can get fresh water from the sea, which gives me
hope that genius, say, and mind, and
the fact that she does not reject me wholly
will find me Joy someday.
Nothing else can quell
or allay this fire.

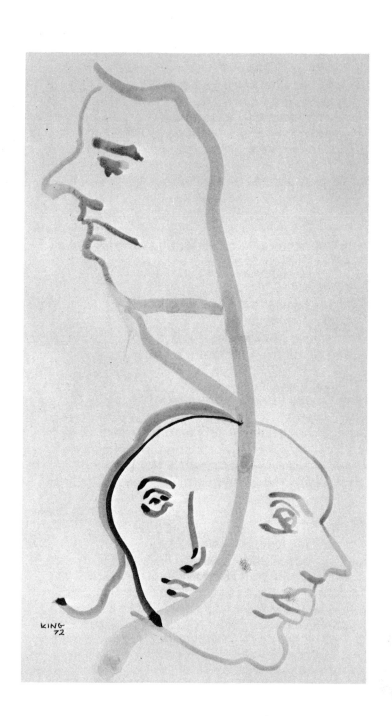

Lady cure me, don't
stand and watch me die, a Lazarus,
                        of this sweet sickness.
My running away from it's no good,
            my eyes play tricks.
When I leave
I see your beauty before me upon all the roads,
            can neither go
                        nor go back.
May I die accursed in hell
if I had the whole world, but lacked
you

and things stood well.

Drogoman senher, s'agues bon destrier

Lord Expositor, if I had a horse
my enemies would be really up the creek.
Even now they get sick when they hear my name called out
                 like quails
        hearing the cry of a sparrow hawk.
        They value their lives not a denier
      they know I am that savage,
      that fierce.

And when I have my double-hauberk on
                and gird on
      the sword Sir Guy gave me not long since,
the earth shakes, there where I walk,
and no enemy of mine is so presumptuous that
         he will not yield immediately
               the right of way.
They're that afraid to hear my step upon the highroad.

      In boldness, Roland & Oliver are my match,
      in gallantry, Bernard de Montdidier.
          And I have found
      such renown in tourney that
             messengers
      come to me in batches, each
          with a ring of gold
            on a black-and-white silk cord
      along with such greetings as rejoice my heart.

All ways I have the semblance of a parfait knight
             which is true,
and I know of Love all his mastery and all
things that pertain to being lover.
          I swear,
you've never seen one in chamber more agreeable, nor
          with arms in hand

more sobering and powerful.
Ladies who've never seen me love and fear.

And if I had a horse,
a good corsair,
the king would live serene near Balaguier,
and fall into a soft sleep undisturbed.
For I'd keep the peace in Provence
                    and Montpellier,
                    and'd give my vow
that brigands and highwaymen would not despoil
                    Autaves nor the Crau.

And if the king turn from the sea to-
                    ward Toulouse,
and the count comes out with his mangy pikemen
                    who cry all day in Gascon
            "ASPE! ORSAU!"
        I vaunt that the first blow that falls
shall be my blow.
I'll lay about me so that they'll retreat
at double time for sure into the town,
                    and I along with 'em
if they don't let the damned portcullis down . . .

And if I reach those cuckolds and slanderers who
            with falsity
                    put down another's triumph
            and strike down joy in open and in secret,
they'll know for real what are the blows I measure!
                    Their bodies,
                    were they made of iron or steel,
        will not be worth a god-damned peacock's feather!

Vierna, from Montpellier I send my best,
and Rainier, may you love this knight, for which
my joy is increased by you, thanks be to Christ.

Tant ai longamen cercat

Long I looked for what I did not need, then
I unclenched my hand
and there, that sunlight lay on it,
                    how I do not know.
It came at my bidding lightly and
lightly I took as I desired
                    but now
the granted and given and grown-in-use
I have lost by blundering, misused,
have not gained it
and my friends laugh.

Ah Senher, dear Castiat,
                    I die of this villainy!
for my deadly enemy can
                    wound me with beauty.
Yet I hope for such good recompense,
from pain of love sweet deliverance
                    and end of guile.
But were it not so great a sin to despair . . .

                    But perhaps I speak foolishly
                    with my famous excess of levity
                    yet may be pardoned for it,
                    being so much the fool
                    that the whole world can see it,
                    how I yield to her caprice
                    and venture any emprize
                    if she so will.

My love without frontier
still she finds fault!
and knowing well what she does
seeks how to give me hurt.

I find no love in her
nor a loving heart
nor any warm decision or tender gain.
I cry mercy and mercy does not come,
I cry mercy and dare turn nowhere else.

Yet doubt is a major party to it here,
far from my lady where I sing alone.
And until I have passed the Rhône
                down toward Lombardy
        I will not satisfy my heart
        how things stand there.

No man could look on you and not have joy.
Compassion is the tongue within your mouth
and all there is of mercy is your eyes.
Where I place my strongest hope and all my trust
I acknowledge you my lady,
                and you, my lord,
and send a heart full of warmth and love.

        Vierna, I walk bright in loving you,
        lacking only sight of Castiat, my lord.

Estat ai gran sazo

For a long time I was bitter,
but now am happier than bird in rain or fish in water,
for my lady has sent me a note to tell me
                    "Act like a man, a lover!"
              And I never thought to have her
                    return me to hope again

                   God
                   knows I can't be happy
              unless I return quickly
              to that soft cage her beauty
                   has put me in.
              There it's all softness, warm
              joy, everything courteous.
              Take everything I possess
                   plow it under!
              only to do her pleasure.

So good to look upon the way she's fashioned, her
                   love-shooting eyes, I
              don't know what I'm doing, or
         where I am, she's got me
seized, won, conquered, taken, tied me down, that I
              cannot turn
left, right or away my love or eyes. All I
         have to do is see her—I
                   sing, I'm
              happy with everything.

From the thicket, a flushed bird:
the heart is open to the hunter's arrow.
But a thousand arrows!
and her eyes the bow
and the wound so soft!
Were I next God's throne, lady, and you called

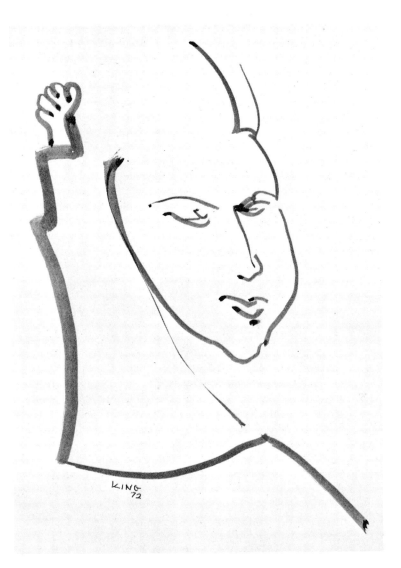

I'd run to you,
willingly rendered and humble,
waiting your mercy and choice.
I live under heavy fear of being
enlaced by a desire for
someone I cannot have. But I
see roses
in ice sheets on the roads,
clear weather
in a sky that's overcast.
Birds sing from the snowdrifts.

But I have a spiteful heart toward one
and wish she'd never lived
since, for a blond count,
she threw me in the road.
Loba!
I think she is a wolf—
she's been taken by a count and
dropped an emperor whose days
all were spent in spreading praise
of her for all the world to hear.
Who lies
does not tell the truth.
A false love's done me in the eye but
I have gained a better lady that way.

God save the illustrious marquis
and his lovely sister,
who with her loyal love has known
how to gently conquer me, and
still more kindly, how to keep me.

I have no walled castle
and my land's not worth two gloves,
but I am lover.

A per pauc de chantar no · m lais

Near to disgust, close to calling quits with song
seeing youth and courage dead
and honest worth that cannot feed itself, for
all men knock it down and boot it out—
wickedness in power that squats
                              on the world's chest
                    and stuffs its mouth with lies—
scarcely a country where one's head
                    is safe from their traps.

The pope, then, and false doctors of the Church,
Christ Jesus, may they live in his anger!
                    selling Rome short:
          such damn fools and liars that
the heretics sing in the streets.
And because these start the lie
it's a hard thing for one to go otherwise, and
I don't look for fights.

Fear out of France and from those
                    who used to be straight,
for their king is not honest or sincere
                    toward man's honor or God's.
The Holy Sepulcher treated as so much real estate!
He does business like a damned bourgeois to the
dishonor of these French.

That stink you breathe is a world that stinks to heaven.
The stench was painful yesterday?
                              Smell it today!
Since the emperor broke from God's goodness
we have not heard of his power increasing,
                    nor his honor,
                    nor knightly prowess. And now
if the fool leaves Richard to rot in his prison, the
                    English will have their say.

The kings of Spain
give me a general pain.
They intrigue for war among themselves.
So now they're sending horses
iron grays and bays
to the Moors, out of fear:
whereupon their pride is doubled,
whereupon they are cut to pieces.
And if some peace were made among them,
some law and trust established—
but Christ knows that would give them no pleasure. . . .

O, when the rich turn crooked
let no man think I am humbled by them!
I am led by a precious joy that is born in me,
holds me rejoicing.
Her love sharp and certain,
clear coming in pleasure,
arms wide in rejoicing.
You're curious?
Do your asking in Carcassonne.

Never sham
never dissimulation
never counterfeit of speech
(a coin ringing true)
never bamboozling friends with a veil
or the chicanery of rouge,
but her own clear color
rising fresh
as an Easter rose.
She is prime above all other beauty, has
joined her youth with wisdom.
The most courtly take pleasure in her company,
speak with all praise the quality of her favour.

NOTES

VIDA and *RAZOS*:

Saint Gilles (Gard).

Alazaïs de Rocamartina (Roquemartine, the ruins thereof, is NW of Aix, about halfway toward Avignon) of the Porcellet family was the first wife of Raimon Gaufridi Barral, viscount of Marseille, who put her aside some time before 1191; he died himself in 1192. Alazais (or Azalaïs; Fr., Adélaide) lived in the vicinity of Arles until 1201 (**Stroński**).

"... until he went overseas with **King Richard**": no secondary sources to substantiate this, though there are sympathetic references to Coeur de Lion in *a per pauc de chantar no·m lais,* written while Richard was captive of the Hohenstaufen Roman Emperor Henry VI (1193-94), and after his release in *Ben viu a gran dolor.* In 1201 or 1202 Peire composed a crusade song, *Baros Jesus qu'en crotz fo mes,* and was evidently on Malta in 1204 or 1205 (*Neus ni gels ni ploja ni fanh*). This latter would have been the 4th crusade, that disgrace, not the 3rd in which Richard was central.

March 25, 1199, at the siege of Châlus, Richard caught a shaft from a strongbow in the shoulder below the nape and near his spine. When the garrison of Châlus had surrendered, Richard interviewed his slayer, pardoned him, and died on the 6th of April. The head of the arrow had gone so deep it could not be removed.

Les Bauz (Baux): near Arles and Tarascon—some of the most impressive ruins in Provence.

"in grief over the death of the good count . . .": Raimon V of Toulouse, d. 1194. The long list of Catalan and Aragonese knights who accompanied Alfons suggests that the biographer might have been Catalan.

La Loba: from one of the *razos* on Raimon de Miraval, another of the several troubadours who sang this lady:

But he loved a lady of Carcassonne who was called Loba de Pennautier, the daughter of en Raimon de Pennautier, and who was married to a rich and powerful knight of Le Cabardès . . . (follows a description of the lady) and all the valorous men and noble barons of the area who met her fell in love with her: the count of Foix, en Oliviers de Saissac, en Peire Rotgiers de Mirepoix, en Aimeric de Montréal, and en Peire Vidal who made many good cansos for her.

Ma domna Estefania: the wife of Bernart d'Alion, the lord of Son (the castle of Donezan near Foix, Ariège, in the Basses-Pyrénées). She is referred to by the *senhal* Bels Sembelis in *Ges pel temps fer e brau* and *De chantar m'era laissatz*, neither of which is in this selection from Vidal's fifty-odd pieces. The standard edition is Joseph Anglade's.

Ma domna Raimbauda de Biolh (Alpes-Maritimes): Peire Vidal sings this lady in *Tart mi veiran mei amic en Tolosa* (my version in Angel Flores' *Anthology of Medieval Lyrics,* The Modern Library, 1962) and again in *De chantar m'era laissatz.* "The ladies of Biolh" show up in what seems to be a much earlier piece, *En una terra estranha*:

> God keep the ladies of Biolh
> for, in them are worth and valor,
> joy, solace, and love, all beauty
>   and all pleasure, all
> of lovely intelligence and knowing.
> When God sees all the virtues in them
> surely he'll place them next him.

". . . the king had arms made for himself and for Peire Vidal and had clothes made for both of them . . .": see paragraph 2 of *razo* I, where Alazaïs also presents him with arms "and they dressed alike." These signs of particular intimacy, wherein here evidence that they took place between lover and lady as well as between men friends, are strikingly parallel to blood-brother rituals. Whole area for investigation of this relationship. The blood relationship in this sense has always been considered the next important to marriage in intimacy and the specific binding of individuals to one another.

Plus qu·l paubres que jatz el ric ostal:

The Lord of Excideuil: Richard Coeur de Lion.

Geoffrey: Richard's brother, Geoffrey Plantagenet, count of Brittany.

Bel Castiat: The identity of most *senhals* cannot be proved absolutely. But there are likelihoods given various internal evidence in the songs, in the *vidas* and *razos* when they are not totally deduced from the songs themselves, and occasional secondary sources such as documents with dates and names and places. Castiat and Vierna are names which appear more often in Vidal's *tornadas* than any others. For Castiat, Bartsch proposed Olivier de Saissac or Aimeric de Montréal; Anglade thinks Raimon V, count of Toulouse (1148-1194) more likely. So do I.

Vierna: it seems very likely that this name designates Alazaïs de Rocamartina, wife of Barral of Marseille. In *Drogoman senher*, where there are clearly disparaging references to the count of Toulouse, the *tornada* is addressed to Vierna and Rainier (Barrals). In *Bels amics cars, ven s'en vas vos estius*, where the *tornada* is dedicated to both Vierna and to Castiat, we can note the separation in space between Peire's two favorite people:

> *Na Vierna, tornar e remaner*
> *Volgra ves vos, si m'en dones lezer*
> *Mos Castiatz, mas trop se fai temer.*

> Vierna, I'd want to come back
> and be with you if my Castiat
> would give me leisure to do so.
> Guess he's too afraid I'll stay

The four kings of Spain: the kings of Castille, Aragon, Navarre and León; certainly Alfons VIII of Castille (1158-1214) and Alfons IX of León (1188-1230); the other two would depend upon a fairly precise dating of the poem. It would seem to be during his exile from Marseille—perhaps he spent part of it traveling through Spain, not just sitting in Genoa as the *razo* suggests? The references to Richard and Geoffrey seem polite though full of praise, without the feeling of warmth and intimacy that might have been there had they shared the planks of a ship together. Which might date the piece before the 3rd crusade, i.e., prior to the summer of 1190. In that case, it would be Alfons II of Aragon (1162-1196) and Sancho VI of Navarre (1150-1194). Coeur de Lion married Sancho's daughter, Berengaria, the summer of 1190 in Limassol on Cyprus, en route to Palestine. If the piece is later than I think, the monarchs might have been Pedro II of Aragon (1196-1213) and Sancho VII of Navarre (1194-1234).

Anglade says that the latest we can date any poem of Peire's is 1205, so that he may not have lived to see his good advice taken. The kingdom of León stayed out of it, but Sancho VII was with Alfons VIII of Castille and Alfons II of Aragon at the battle of Las Navas de Tolosa, July 16, 1212, which broke the back of the Mohammedan power in Spain. Yakub al-Mansur, emir of the Almohades, was the losing pitcher.

Una canso ai faita mortamen:

"the squire who died at table": No one knows who he was; figure from a romance we've lost ?

"May I die accursed in hell . . .": Vidal is sometimes thought to have flirted with heresy. It seems unlikely somehow.

Drogoman senher, s'agues bon destrier:

Drogoman, the Lord Expositor: Anglade suggests the count of Toulouse; how? The piece seems clearly anti-Toulousain and pro-Aragonese. My vote is for Guillem VIII, marquis de Montpellier and the *tornada* sends his regards specifically from that city. (G. de Montpellier died in 1202). Another possibility is Sancho, son of the king of Aragon, who governed (held forth?) in his name in Provence (1181-85). Anyway, Peire seems to have been in some trouble at the court of the count of Toulouse, hometown boy makes good, etc.

50

Sir Guy: Gui de Lusignan, whom he might have met on crusade?

"the king would live serene . . .": Alfons II of Aragon; Balaguer (Balaguier) is a Catalan town.

Aspe and Orsau: two towns in the Basses-Pyrénées.

Estat ai gran sazo:

There were so many good things in this *canso* that I hated to scrap it because of an equally heavy load of clichés: nor would a simple cutting and reordering of the continuity pull it together. A solution appeared when I remembered a number of isolated lines, stanzas, individual images scattered throughout Vidal's whole chansonnier of about 50 pieces, which had pricked my imagination in the reading, but did not seem at the time sufficient motive to undertake the whole piece. I should like to indicate these intercalations and the sources of each. The references are to Anglade's edition.

"From the thicket . . . soft! " has two sources: p. 38, XIII(*v*): 32-35;

> *Plus que l'auzels qu'es noiritz lai per Fransa,*
> *Quant hom l'apel' et el respon coitos*
> *E sap qu'es mortz, paus mon cor voluntos*
> *Als mils cairels qu'ab sos bels olhs mi lansa.*

and p. 24, IX(*iii*): 18-19;

> *E son cairel el cor mis;*
> *et anc mais colps tan no · m plac . . .*

"But I see roses . . . overcast": p. 47, XVI(*i*): 9-10;

> *Paro m rozas entre gel*
> *E clars temps ab trebol cel.*

And that bird was still with me. "I have no walled castle . . . lover":
p. 7, III(*iv*): 25-28;

> *Non ai castel serrat de mur*
> *Ni ma terra no val dos gans,*
> *Mas anc no fo plus fis amans*
> *De mi . . .*

Since there will be no second opportunity, I'd like to offer here a few other Peire Vidal passages which got to me—ones I did not interpolate. Two of them gloss the rules and conditions of courtly love; the rest I give solely for their own qualities.

p. 6, III(*iii*): 17-18;

> *De clartat m'a mes en escur*
> *Cela per cui vauc dezirans*
>
> Because of her
> I have passed from the clear light into shadow.

p. 7, III(*iii*): 21-24; on waiting to attain that stage where the lover is permitted the intimacy of looking upon his lady naked:

> *Mas be·us dic que tan sofrirai,*
> *Tro posca en loc avenir,*
> *Qu'ab mos olhs son bel cors remir,*
> *E s'i aura trop al meu par.*
>
> But let me tell you how much I'll suffer
> before I may come to that place where
>   I may look upon
>   with my own eyes
>   her lovely body
> and that as far as I'm concerned, it
>   will seem too long.

p. 33, XI(*vii*): 55-57; on the liars and talebearers:

> *Plus que no pot ses aiga viure· l peis,*
> *No pot esser ses lauzengier domneis,*
> *Per qu'amador compron trop car lor joc.*

> A fish cannot live without water,
> nor love at court be without liars,
> so lovers buy their joy too dearly.

p. 18, VII(*v*): 29-30;

> *Doncs car tan l'am, mout sui plus folatura*
> *Que fols pastres qu'a bel poi caramela.*

> I have gone half-cracked, I have loved her so,
>   am crazier than the
>   the mad herdsman
>   at his reed
>   on the soft hillside.

p. 22, VIII(*v*): 49-53;

> *Quar plus qu'obra d'aranha*
>   *Non pot aver durada*
>   *Amors, pos es proada,*
>   *Qu'ab ditz daur' et aplanha*
> *Tal qu'a· l cor de vilan escolh*

> Love is a spider's web for delicacy,
> and will last about as long
> if a man be not true.

"Were I next God's throne, lady, and you called . . .": more food for the heresy charge against Vidal.

"She's been taken by a count . . .": Loba's lover seems to have been Roger, count of Foix (1188-1223).

"the illustrious marquis and his lovely sister": Boniface I, marquis of Montferrat. His sister Alazaïs married Manfred II, marquis of Saluces in 1182.

53

A per pauc de chantar no· m lais:

The year of this *sirventes* seems to be 1193. Coeur de Lion (see stanza *iv*) is still in a German prison; Celestine III is Pope; papal legates and missions of preachers and bishops are wandering the south getting decrees passed against the Catharists and extorting recantations and public penances from wealthy heretics under the threat of confiscation of their worldly goods; Phillipe-Auguste of France is intriguing with Henry Hohenstaufen, the Holy Roman Emperor to keep the English king prisoner in the fortress chamber at Trifels; and doubtless with the papacy to keep pressure on the good count Raimon of Toulouse, the stronghold of heresy, in return for certain concessions in the Holy Land; Raimon V, meanwhile, is up to his eyebrows in Alfons II's renewal of hostilities with the Touslousain, Aragon having as allies Pere Lara, viscount of Narbonne and Raymond Roger, count of Foix. Raimon V, Peire Vidal's lord (*Mos Castiatz*), will die this next year, though Richard will be released in February at Mainz when the politicking and the ransoming have ended.

But 1193 is a bad year, and no one knows the good news or the bad news of 1194. Things are no better in Spain, with wars among the Christian kings still raging, and many years of retaking Valencia and defeats (Yakub al-Mansur will give Alfons VIII a good drubbing at Alarcos in La Mancha in July 1195) still ahead.

The last two stanzas to Loba de Pennautier come as something of a relief. What the hell, ro-mance!

54

SELECTED BIBLIOGRAPHY

Included in this bibliography are all works Paul Blackburn cites in his notes.

Texts

Anglade, Joseph, ed. *Les poésies de Peire Vidal*, 2nd ed. Les classiques français du moyen âge, no. 11. Paris, 1966.

Bartsch, Karl, ed. *Chrestomathie provençale*, 6th ed. rev. Eduard Koschwitz. Marburg, 1904.

Blackburn, Paul. *Proensa*. Divers Press, Palma de Mallorca, Spain, 1953.

Flores, Angel, ed. *Anthology of Medieval Lyrics*. Modern Library, 330. New York, 1962.

Studies

Dronke, Peter. *The Medieval Lyric*. New York, 1968.

Economou, George. "Test of Translation X: Guillem Comte de Peitau's *Ab la dolchor del temps novel*," *A Caterpillar Anthology*, Clayton Eshleman, ed. New York, 1971.

Goldin, Frederick. *The Mirror of Narcissus in the Courtly Love Lyric*. Ithaca, 1967.

Hoepffner, Ernest. *Le troubadour Peire Vidal*. Paris, 1961.

——————. *Les troubadours dans leur vie et dans leur oeuvres*. Paris, 1955.

Klein, Karen W. *The Partisan Voice, A Study of the Political Lyric in France and Germany, 1180-1230*. The Hague and Paris, 1971.

Stroński, S. *Le troubadour Folquet de Marseille*. Cracow, 1910.

Valency, Maurice. *In Praise of Love*. New York, 1958.

George Economou